SIPPING TEA IN THE LIVING ROOM

SIPPING TEA IN THE LIVING ROOM

DESIGNED FOR LIFE

MASTERPIECES IN THE
MASTER'S HAND

T. T. CAROLE

Table of Contents

INTRODUCTION

     Gentle readers please allow me to introduce myself. I am a frustrated interior designer—divinely gifted, greatly impassioned, well-educated and purposefully trained in the fantastic field of interior design. Frustrated (the 'F' word) because after venturing out and building a thriving part-time business and working out my passion in the wonderful, fun and sometimes wacky world of design I allowed self-doubt to enter my head then heart, which caused me to scramble back into hiding in a comfortable, quasi-secure position in the complicated, yet rewarding, world of corporate America. This is where I sit proudly with no regrets.

"No regrets?" You ask. "But wait a minute; didn't I just read a few sentences above that you said that you are frustrated?" Yes, dear reader, you read it correctly. The 'F' word was used but only in the sense that, that part of my life has not been totally fulfilled; yet, I have much for which to be extremely grateful and therefore, so much more to share.

This then effects the motivation for writing such a book as this in this fingertip world. Fingertip because it seems that all that there is for the eyes to see the brain to imagine, and the ears to hear is accessible through a diverse web of high-speed technology and a 24/7 news cycle—or is it?

What about human experiences? What about the human energy and spirit? What about the promises of God? What about, simply, the art of living and being conscientious about all of what is working together to bring us to where we are today?

We each occupy our own *living room* in this life and in this sense; it is more than a physical space or our physical body.

Our living room of life encompasses our thoughts, desires, emotions, beliefs, talents, skills, abilities, weaknesses, and a myriad of our other shared human characteristics, traits, and persona.

It is where we communicate and demonstrate to the world not only who we are but also who we believe we are created to be.

By exposition, we are created in the image of God—"fearfully and wonderfully made" (Psalm 139). Therefore, just as we take the time and make the investment to beautify our physical space for our own pleasure, shouldn't we invest that, and even more in this once in a lifetime experience?

By Divine providence, we have landed in this place called life. We have landed in our living room—a space that is exclusively designated for and is on loan to each of us individually.

It is mortgage and rent-free (Jesus paid the price once and for all). All we must do is make improvements where needed and fill it with the things that glorify the Father. So where do we start?

It is often said that those who can; do and those who cannot; teach.

My dear reader, I would like to spin that web of words into something much more hopeful such as this: 'Until you can do, share all that you know and all that you do with as many of those who think that they cannot, until they believe that they can'.

With this book, I would like to do that and more, even if you already believe you can. In fact, to facilitate this, enlisted here is some expert advice, lifted from the **B**est **I**nterior **B**eautification **L**esson **E**ver. However, these lessons do not come without a cost. The charge is to rely solely on self, less and submit to the leanings of the Spirit of God, more.

Even now, as I am developing and evolving in my total experiences and seeking to share with you, I slip into that phase of questioning way too much and leaning way too little. Then comes that moment when that sweet whisper beckons me to sit at His feet and listen to the voice of my Creator.

My conversations with Him are far too intimate and passionate to repeat and excessively personal to reveal—all at once, that is. Therefore, I have done my best to creatively spin them into reflections, anecdotes, and lessons learned on life's journey while cleverly pairing the delightful art of interior design with the beautiful heart of God.

From my living room of life, I see the Beauty of God all around—even in some of the oddest art or in our most curious circumstances. I am not saying that I believe that God, himself, is in the art, but I do believe that He created the person and the means to create the art.

Similarly, I do not believe that God causes the tangled messes in which might sometimes land, but I do believe that He is ever-present and operating in those situations to cause things to work out for His glory and our good.[i]

As you join me in my living room of life, you will be able to make my stories, observations and other lessons learned your own by integrating each with your own experiences.

You might begin thinking things like: "I thought that only happened to me". Maybe, "I was thinking the same thing". On the other hand, simply, "I didn't know you could do it that way".

You might even find yourself asking questions like: "What would I have done in that situation?" Similarly, "Why would anyone do it that way?" Alternately, "Why not do it this way?"

At any rate, when you walk away from this unique and dual experiment of living room design, hopefully you will be inspired to find new appreciation for the way that life happens all around you.

At the same time, you will be well on your way, (armed with generous DIY tips, tricks of the trade, and design expertise) to creating or adding touches to your natural living space that will make it a special place in your home for your family and you.

CHAPTER 1

THE LIVING ROOM

I remember growing up in the heart of the city. We lived on a tree-lined, private street, in a modest two-story, brick home (which housed a large and sometimes extended family). The neighborhood was energetic and bustling with activities—where children are playing; the Mr. Softie or bomb pop truck's music is blasting from its speakers in an attempt to sway a sale; and grown-ups sitting on the porch, in yard chairs, or talking over the fence to one another about whatever was in the news.

I remember the house very well and that aside from the kitchen (and of course the bedrooms and bath), that the living room—neatly tucked behind a pair of pocket doors on the right side as you enter into the hallway—was the most important room of the house. I remember it at its best and its worst.

I remember the living room being the gathering spot for the family and where friends would settle in whenever they would come to visit. My parents were social people and very active in the church—where we enjoyed great community. Couple that with the fact that dad was a Sunday school superintendent, teacher, and deacon; mom was in the choir, on the Mothers Board, and a great cook and you get a lot of activity.

I remember the living room decorated for holidays, surprise birthday parties, cake walks (definitely a church activity) and many other joyous occasions. Alternately, I also remember it as a place of mourning and sorrow whenever there was bad news to share— whether an illness or death of a loved one. We all gathered there, in the living room, to support each other, and to process the news and sort things out.

I remember the living room tastefully decorated and well appointed, as well as it stripped to the studs as a work in progress. I remember it, at times, looking pristine (with white furniture covered with clear vinyl slipcovers covers) as well as it at times a bit cluttered because somebody did not keep up with their chores.

Digging a little deeper, however, I realize that there is another very important something that I remember about the living room. I remember that whenever the living room was at its best—thoroughly cleaned and bedecked with fine furnishing, my mom, with good reason, laid down the law declaring that the room was off limits: no food, no drinks, and no horsing around.

As kids, we came to understand that these boundaries were set to protect and preserve the room while it was in such a beautiful state. It was obvious to us, even then, that whenever folk would come to visit, the living room served not only as a witness of my parents' sacrifice and provision for us but also as a sign that the family was doing okay. I think this is why I can say that the living room was a very important part of our home.

Fast forward to today. I'm all grown up with a home of my own and am not the least bit surprised by the fact that the living room in my home looks very pleasant to me. However, unlike when I was growing up, my living room (except for a holiday or two once or twice a year) is not bustling with activity and there are no rules. Yet today (just like then), I experience my living room when it is festively adorned, clean, decked out, pristine, cluttered, bare, and in various stages of repair and disrepair. And here too, is where I am bound to experience every emotion from laughter to tears; anxiety to reassurance; from disappointment to satisfaction; passion to indifference; from anger to calm;

regret to contentment; from joy to sorrow—and the list goes on.

If I would dare to psycho-analyze myself and dig a little deeper, I would boldly assert that the living room in my home is much like my life—a combination and sum of my life's station, status, and situations.

When you walk into the living room of my home, you would probably be able to make some very safe assumptions and statements about me such as, "She likes orange." Maybe, "She likes books or loves to read". Moreover, "There definitely aren't any kids in this house".

Your assumptions and opinions would reflect the things with which I surround myself and how you evaluate and interpret those things that you see.

Similarly, were we to meet outside of home and I were to conduct myself in a certain way towards or around you. Or, were I to share with you some of my flippant views, deepest thoughts or darkest secrets, then based on those and how you evaluate and interpret the same, you then too, would have a basis on which to form an opinion.

I believe that the spaces that we create or develop around ourselves—both physically and dynamically— are reflections of who we are and of how and for whom we live.[ii]

My living room (physically and internally) is my own little corner of the whole, wide world. This is where and how I live.

Your Personal Style: A Quick Quiz

Assessing and rearranging our living rooms should not be a casual encounter; in fact, it should be a very intimate affair. That is why it is extremely necessary to have the proper input, guidance, and tools to help throughout the process.

Some amazing tools that I would suggest are the Bible (in an easily readable and understandable version); great books by good and sound authors; prayer & meditation; input from trusted family, friends and/or professionals; and a healthy, balanced mix of an open heart, teachable mind and willing spirit.

To Thine Own Self be True"

William Shakespeare, in his much-acclaimed stage play, Hamlet, coined the well-known and often used quote: "This above all: to thine own self be true…"

This is at a point in the play where Polonius lends advice to his son, Laertes as Laertes is leaving for a trip to Paris.

Polonius continues, "…it must follow, as the night the day, thou canst not then be false to any man/Farewell, my blessing season this in thee!"

While the contemporary treatment of the quote shows up everywhere from training and teambuilding exercises in the corporate world to the world of creative arts and human science, there is much discussion in the literary world about what exactly did he mean when Polonius spoke these words to Laertes.

Some suggest that Polonius' was advising Laertes to be loyal to himself and to always look out for his own best interests. Some suggest that he was advising Laertes to do all of the right things and judge himself first then others will judge him accordingly. Yet, others believe Polonius was admonishing Laertes to always be honest in his ways and relations.

I believe that depending on what it is that we are trying to accomplish, any of these explanations could apply. However, the one of which I am most fond is the one that closely mirrors the wisdom of Apostle Paul to Timothy.

Paul admonished Timothy to flee from behaviors, thoughts and actions such as envy, controversy, bath-mouthing, rumors, and the love of money that might contaminate his witness and to fervently pursue and holdfast to a life full of wonder, faith, love, steadiness and courtesy, for which he was known.[iii]

What a Wacky Nest

Growing up, many of us had the opportunity to learn from many books, poems, and plays while making our way through preschool, grade school, middle school and beyond. However, during those years when we were working for a 'Good' grade and report card, we might have lacked the maturity to realize the relevant revelations in plain sight. We did not recognize the invaluable inspiration and encouragement that passed through our fingertips. As life would have it, it is not until we grow up and go through some things (if we are lucky) that we are able to recall and apply a tidbit of the vast amount of wisdom and knowledge of which we were an audience.

The collection of Aesop's Fables is a perfect example of a desired and celebrated body of wisdom. I recently researched and found that there are more than 650 stories alone in the collection. However, one that I recall then researched for a time such as this is one chronicling an eye-opening encounter between a covetous, confused, conflicted crow, travelers in a wilderness, and a cool, confident, clever raven.

In this familiar yarn, the crow noticed that the raven was enjoying many accolades and celebrations by men because many of them, as explorers, looked to and relied on the raven's ability to cleverly signal signs and warnings while guiding them to safety during their treks in the wild, woods of sometimes unknown or desolate places.

By God's design, at least in this case, this particular crow was simply not gifted in the same way as the raven—she was probably gifted in other ways and purposed for other things, yet undoubtedly she seemed to lack the appreciation for and understanding of this fact.

Yet with each adventure, the crow grudgingly studies the travelers, watches the raven, and hears the accolades to the point of becoming overwhelmed, maddened, and wrecked by the germs of envy.

As the crow's jealousy continued to get the best of her, and resentment proceeded to transmute into rage, the crow flew high up into the trees to imitate the raven. She desperately yearned for their attention and wished that the travelers would delight in her, too, and celebrate her just as they did the raven.

As the tale goes, when the trekkers approached, the crow, high up in the trees, seized the opportunity and she cawed. Each time she cawed, she cawed more energetically and more loudly than before.

The men, however, were more annoyed than impressed. They did not regard her machinations to be an omen as she (in an attempt to stir their imaginations), cawed as loudly as she could. The men simply dismissed her flailing as noise and pointed out the fact that the bird was not a clever raven but merely a common crow, and they thought her cawing to be ridiculous.

The apparent moral of the story is this: **Those who assume a character which does not belong to them, only make themselves ridiculous."**

Therefore, to avoid the embarrassment of the crow, it might serve us well to invest in real, honest, and sober self-assessment of ourselves so that we can come to a place where we can acknowledge and admire others for their contributions while at the same time, doing the best at whatever it is that we were made to do.

An honest and sober self-assessment could, indeed, make us better stewards in our living room of this precious gift of life by helping us to better understand, expose, improve upon and be who we are meant to be.

The Quiz: Take it, sure; but not too seriously

The following quiz is allegedly a tool of a famous talk show host and TV personality. I cannot speak to its reliability because no one has claimed to be its author. It just lingers in the Cloud, and is memorialized on the Web, and passed around on Facebook.

Though this quiz is fun, some might find it somewhat challenging because it arouses the tendency of trying to analyze the questions to determine just what the question is trying to assess.

If you are anything like me, you might manage to get through this one without much analysis by heeding the advice to read the question and quickly pick what you believe is the most honest and best answer about yourself

Never the less, what is essential and important to understand as we proceed to the quiz is that no matter the score, the good news is that God can and will use any and every created body and thing to accomplish His goals as He works everything out for His glory and our good.

So, grab a pen and paper, and let us get started. Be as honest with yourself as you possibly can. Moreover, have fun!

The answer key can be found immediately following the assessment.

1. When do you feel your best?
a) in the morning
b) during the afternoon & and early evening
c) late at night

2. You usually walk
a) fairly fast, with long steps
b) fairly fast, with little steps
c) less fast head up, looking the world in the face
d) less fast, head down
e) very slowly

3. When talking to people you
a) stand with your arms folded
b) have your hands clasped
c) have one or both your hands on your hips
d) touch or push the person to whom you are talking
e) play with your ear, touch your chin, or smooth your hair

4. When relaxing, you sit with
a) your knees bent with your legs neatly side by side
b) your legs crossed

c) your legs stretched out or straight

d) one leg curled under you

5. When something really amuses you, you react with

a) a big, appreciative laugh

b) a laugh, but not a loud one

c) a quiet chuckle

d) a sheepish smile

6. When you go to a party or social gathering

a) make a loud entrance so everyone notices you

b) make a quiet entrance, looking around for someone you know

c) make the quietest entrance, trying to stay unnoticed

7. You're working very hard, concentrating hard, and you're interrupted; do you ...

a) welcome the break

b) feel extremely irritated

c) vary between these two extremes

8. Which of the following colors do you like most?

a) Red or orange

b) black

c) yellow or light blue

d) green

e) dark blue or purple

f) white

g) brown or gray

9. When you are in bed at night, in those last few moments before going to sleep, you lie

a) stretched out on your back

b) stretched out face down on your stomach

c) on your side, slightly curled

d) with your head on one arm

e) with your head under the covers

10. You often dream that you are

a) falling

b) fighting or struggling

c) searching for something or somebody

d) flying or floating

e) you usually have dreamless sleep

f) your dreams are always pleasant

POINTS: Pick the corresponding points for your answer to each question.

1. (a) 2 (b) 4 (c) 6

2. (a) 6 (b) 4 (c) 7 (d) 2 (e) 1

3. (a) 4 (b) 2 (c) 5 (d) 7 (e) 6

4. (a) 4 (b) 6 (c) 2 (d) 1

5. (a) 6 (b) 4 (c) 3 (d) 5 (e) 2
6. (a) 6 (b) 4 (c) 2
7. (a) 6 (b) 2 (c) 4
8. (a) 6 (b) 7 (c) 5 (d) 4 (e) 3 (f) 2 (g) 1
9. (a) 7 (b) 6 (c) 4 (d) 2 (e) 1
10. (a) 4 (b) 2 (c) 3 (d) 5 (e) 6 (f) 1

Now add up the total number of points.

OVER 60 POINTS: Others see you as someone they should "handle with care". You are seen as vain, self-centered, and who is extremely dominant. Others may admire you, wishing they could be more like you, but do not always trust you, hesitating to become too deeply involved with you.

51 TO 60 POINTS: Others see you as an exciting, highly volatile, rather impulsive personality; a natural leader, who is quick to make decisions, though not always the right ones. They see you as bold and adventuresome, someone who will try anything once; someone who takes chances and enjoys an adventure. They enjoy being in your company because of the excitement your radiate.

41 TO 50 POINTS: Others see you as fresh, lively, charming, amusing, practical, and always interesting; someone who is constantly in the center of attention, but sufficiently well-balanced not to let it go to their head.

They also see you as kind, considerate, and understanding; someone who will always cheer them up and help them out.

31 TO 40 POINTS: Others see you as sensible, cautious, careful & practical. They see you as clever, gifted, or talented, but modest. Not a person who makes friends too quickly or easily, but someone who's extremely loyal to friends you do make and who expect the same loyalty in return. Those who really get to know you realize it takes a lot to shake your trust in your friends, but equally that it takes you a long time to get over it if that trust is ever broken.

21 TO 30 POINTS: Your friends see you as painstaking and fussy. They see you as very cautious, extremely careful, a slow and steady plodder. It would really surprise them if you ever did something impulsively or on the spur of the moment, expecting you to examine everything carefully from every angle and then, usually decide against it. They think this reaction is caused partly by your careful nature.

UNDER 21 POINTS: People think you are shy, nervous, and indecisive, someone who needs looking after, who always wants someone else to make the decisions & who does not want to get involved with anyone or anything. They see you as a worrier who always sees problems that do not exist. Some people

think you are boring. Only those who know you well
know   that   you   are   not.

CHAPTER 3

Know What You Are Working With

My nephew Charles was born with Down's syndrome. I consider getting to know and love him one of the great privileges and honor in my life. As he was growing up, he was lovingly dubbed Lil' Charles.

I first met Lil' Charles when he was at the age of five or so. When I met him, it was out of pure ignorance that I could not help but feel sorry for him. I could not help but wonder why the Lord would let him and countless other babies like him come into this beautiful world of great expectations and abundance of opportunities with debilitating disabilities such as this. Why, Lord, why?

However, having since grown in my knowledge and understanding of, both, Lil' Charles and our great big God, I find that I am asking that question now, not so much. It is amazing how exposure to larger than life situations and trust in God can make you a lot smarter.

As I was learning about Lil' Charles's situation and getting to know him, I found that he was a very bright and loving kid. It only took one introduction, a big hug, and a kiss on the forehead, for him never to forget my name and to know me forever more.

Juxtaposed to my ignorance was the wisdom of my dearly beloved mother that allowed her to see not a pitiful, defective, doomed-for-life child, but instead the powerful, wonder working of an all-knowing God.

She saw Lil' Charles as God's blank canvas—as if God, Himself, had shared with her a secret that nobody else could know. She would study Lil' Charles for a while and then would say, "That boy is gonna be somethin' one day."

Yet, for me, ignorance prevailed, and I found that I still looked at Lil' Charles and wondered what she was seeing in him that was different from what I was seeing. I mean, I was born with a creative mind, a visionary. Shouldn't I be able to see or imagine something more magnificent and different?

Many years have passed since that time. I am now overjoyed to say that wisdom has taught me that vision takes more than a creative mind. It also takes experiences—some bought and some taught as some would say—and it takes having an unusual kind of faith that we all will undoubtedly need to guide us through our living room experience.

Lil' Charles, now known as Charlie, is all grown up. Is he a little different? Yes! He looks a little different, talks, and learns differently than most; however, there is no difference in his love and passion for life.

Charlie loves good food, which is an unmistakable fact, considering the girth of his squat build. And, he loves people. No matter how some might view him, he has yet to meet a stranger neither whose hand he will not shake nor person whom he will not embrace.

And, Charlie is quite the entertainer. He loves to participate in family gatherings, where it is no secret that he makes himself the star on the dance floor. He loves the Lord and he loves going to church where his voice rings out above most others as he dances with joy and delivers up a hearty Amen or thank you Lord while celebrating worship.

Another thing that I have come to love about Charlie is that he has a unique approach in taking on assignments and he puts mounds of energy into anything that decides to do.

There was the time during a Mothers' Day celebration at church when he broke loose and let the congregation know just what he was working with.

On this particular Sunday, the all-male choir finished singing one of two songs when the minister of music called for Charlie to come up from the audience. Charlie, with his childlike enthusiasm, ran immediately and took his seat at the drums—not nervous, not shy, and not embarrassed.

As the choir sang their last song, it was somewhere towards the end that the minister of music pointed to Charlie who was by then firmly seated in the music pit.

At that point, Charlie began to beat the drums. He beat; and he beat; and he beat. Charlie beat the drums with so much energy and fervor that the choir was no longer the focus; Charlie was the man of the hour.

Tat, diddy, tat, diddy, bang, diddy, tat, tat, diddy, clang, clang, clang of the cymbals. Charlie—by the time his stint was over, the reverberation and the rat-a-tat-tat of the drums and clang of the cymbals had subsided—

had joyfully succeeded in bringing the entire congregation to its feet.

The audience had a raucous reaction. Judging by the response, some were apparently amused, some astonished, and some, possibly like me, were simply amazed as we watched and admired his courage.

Then true to his passionate, energetic, and unashamed self, Charlie realized that he was the subject of a standing ovation. He jumped up from his seat, threw his hands in the air jubilantly as he leaped across the floor to the other side of the sanctuary.

This, indeed, was that moment that I realized mom was right. That boy is surely "gonna be something one day."

That was a great revelation that rings true, even to this day. I was truly enlightened and made wiser about the fact that no matter whom or no matter what, our differences lay mainly on the surface of a blank and otherwise very complex, fearfully and wonderfully made canvass.

This canvass is God's workroom and He, indeed, is the Master Designer. He, alone, knows whom and for what purpose we are designed. With or without encumbrances, if we acknowledge Him, he will give us hope and a future.[iv]

When Charlie beat those drums, sure, he was rocking the crowd; however, he was also praising and making music for the Lord Almighty, who made him for that very purpose at that time.

In that moment, I believe that everyone in the place who believed in something or someone bigger than himself or herself sensed the mighty presence of God.

I believe we all possibly walked away with a higher hope that assures us that no matter how painfully barren the canvass might appear to us moment by moment; no matter how desperately clueless or ill formed in our minds, our Sovereign God is carefully coordinating the scenarios.

He will get the glory as He continues to work everything out for our good.[v]

Charlie lives his life. Unlike "normal" people who make it a habit of dealing with all sorts of irrational fears and phobias, he allows himself to be God's blank canvass.

While "normal" folk are whining and finding things to complain about, Charlie seems confident enough to take life in stride and go with the flow.

He has the courage to let go and let the Lord have His way with him.

Nobody should be surprised that his favorite song (which he might belt out at any given moment), is "To God Be the Glory".

I really admire Charlie and am not surprised to know that he has touched, taught, and caused change in the lives of many people that know and love him.

Charlie is not disabled—he is exceptionally enabled and through him, God he has done and will continue to do many exceptional things.

DIY: Tips & Trick of the Trade

A Clean Slate and a Fresh Idea

The ideal way to begin a decorating or design project is to start with a clean slate—an empty room with great bones (structurally sound) or an ability to dismiss everything that you see that is already there.

You must get to know the room: mentally, you have to live in it; you have to walk in it, breathe in it, and listen to it. You will have to take in as much of it as you can as you let the space surround and speak to you its preferences, possibilities, and potential.

Realistically, though, starting from scratch might not always be possible and it certainly might not make sense to some to do so.

Therefore, the best thing to do—even with a fully furnished room—is to start with a clear idea about the look and feel that you are trying to achieve.

Pay attention to what inspires you: colors, furniture styles, pieces of art, or even articles of clothing.

Know your style: do you have a penchant for the relaxed contemporary; favor the coolness of modern; feel drawn to the austerity of the traditional, the hominess of country, or the eclectic look of the shabby chic?

If you are not that familiar with the looks and labels mentioned above, then 'put it in the Google'—as I've heard some say—click on 'images' and see what pops up. Then try to imagine how you would feel coming home day in and day out to that look or something similar.

Here, however, I must caution anyone who seeks to emulate someone else's designs with which you might find yourself smitten.

For me, if my own room or place to be designed is the polar opposite, I should not do myself the disservice of falling in love with the look and feel of a large, well-lit south facing room—which has floor to ceiling Palladian windows; beautiful, bold black walls;

plush white furniture and delightfully measured pops of color all around—and thinking that, that room will work for me.

No. If my house does not have that personality, then the chances of my room being a knockout are slim to none.

I would instead do well to consider the fact that the architect, builder and designer who converged to bring all of that beautiful boldness together for the room for which I am coveting, did so with that level of drama in mind. And, for my own room which might be the opposite, then the possibility of this coming together successfully is probably not so much.

Though it is a given that everybody has a right to do whatever they want in their own space; however the chances are pretty good that making bad decisions, whether consciously or unconsciously, will leave you feeling a bit awkward.

What if our room is small and leaning to the dark side and we relish the thought of that big space drama? Then, a better choice might be, that rather than painting the walls black, do the opposite and paint the walls a light, neutral color and then place a proportionally large, bold, predominantly black trip tic on a south facing wall.

Next, add nicely proportioned furniture—a white sofa and a black chair. Accent by popping in accessories such as pillows, lamps, and smaller accessories in rich red (or other bright bold) color.

Finally, throw in a nice area rug that compliments and picks up the colors, shapes, and textures all around (this will help to ground the room).

Then, voile! Small space—big drama.

CHAPTER 4

The Principles of Design:

Creating and Appreciating Unity & Harmony in the Living Room

The best practice for achieving our personal and finest level of success in creating unity and harmony in the living room of life is embracing and adhering to a well-balanced mixture of some basic and defined principles.

Regardless of artistic choice or standard of living preference, the principles that should be applied remain the same, and they are:

Order – arranging matters in a suitable sequence;

Balance – the distribution of weight or stress;

Scale and proportion – a comparative relationship of size

Contrasts and similarities – comparative difference or resemblances

A well-established focal point – a center or guide; and

A proper perspective – a relatively good point of view.

However, while nothing is absolute, all of these balanced and together help us to realize a different kind of joy and a new appreciation for peace whenever we might we find ourselves immersed in a sundry of scenery or uncomfortable settings that might seem desperately unpleasant, woefully wicked, or just plain ole ugly.

By using the principles and precepts that are set before us, we might find that we are able to renew our mind and transform our living room of life into a different and 'more better' kind of place. Who would not want to live there?

This is the place where when rocked by circumstances, all of the elements that create unity and harmony converge in such a way as to make something that might otherwise overtake us, suddenly seem weirdly charming and able to provide an amazingly provocative life-enriching experience.

It is a place where we take command of our senses and decide the mood that we are going to set and the tone that we are going to take.

It is where we persuade ourselves to replace the mentality of defeatism and doom and gloom, with the power of praise, thanksgiving, optimism, and unspeakable joy.

Moreover, it is a place where we can sit back, relax, enjoy the scenery, kick up our heels, or jump for joy whenever things are going well, or even, dig in our heels, take a stand and stand strong and at peace while in the face of adversity.

This is where we stop sacrificing faithfulness for expediency and realize that we are a work in progress and are building on the promises of a beautifully laid, solid foundation. All while knowing that we are not doing this by ourselves because the joy of the Lord is our strength.[vi]

The alternative of choosing to use the principles for creating unity and harmony in our surroundings is ignoring them and possibly settling for living baselessly, groundlessly, or merely by chance and happenstance in an alternatively, designed space.

While living in this alternative space might seem a prosperous, very exciting, or mind-blowing experience for a very rare few, it would more likely than not provide an unsettling, chaotic, and toxic environment for most others.

This alternative environment is one without a center. It is out of order. It feeds and operates on the fumes of pressure, both, from within and without.

Here in the alternative place, problems will seem disproportionately large and perceptions critically skewed.

Disharmony flourishes and disunity is established.

Moreover, everything seems a bit off; the presence of peace is mystified and in its stead is a still-life medley of a clumsy, muddled mess.

Fortunately, not all is lost in this alternative place of disrepair because there is a fix.

The Fix

Perhaps it is a good idea to point out here that creating and appreciating a well-structured, unified, and harmonious living room of life that will set our spirit free is not an easy task nor should it be a DIY endeavor.

This momentous task requires the Plan of the Architect (found in the Father), the Master Designer (found in Jesus), and the Project Manager (found in the Holy Spirit of God).

It must be said that apart from the Plan, we participate in the process as carpenters with a lot of zeal, but a lack of the understanding or discipline required for following the long-established blueprint.

If left to our own devices, willfully, we hurry up the project here; cut corners there; and even add our own troubled touches.

Then without communicating with the Designer (through prayer and meditation), we stop making the right connections.

Then, before we know it, we are working with the power tools of deceit, malice, and mischief.

We unwittingly start using doubt as our trade manual and impatience as our skill.

However, even when we stray from the Plan (when we choose to impose our own way), The Architect loves us.

His desire for our living room of life to be a reflection of Himself is so great that he tasked Jesus, his Master Designer, with covering mistakes and making everything right before Him.

In addition, he allows His Holy Spirit (in the likeness of a project manager) to continue the work in progress, keeping it secure, and making sure to inspect and expose and bring to our remembrance His well-laid out plans, whenever something is off.

A Snapshot of the Principles in Action Order

Nothing creates order out of chaos better than planning, both, ahead and often. Then, checking your plans.

A few years ago, I planned to take a few days of vacation from work because my family and I were going out of town to attend our family reunion. To prepare, I followed departmental procedures at work, and even though I was planning almost a year ahead of the actual vacation, I checked the calendar to make sure that the Wednesday, Thursday and Friday of that particular week in July were available. Sure enough, those days were available, so by marking my initials on the shared, departmental calendar, I was indicating to my coworkers and managers that I was requesting those days off. By selecting so early, leading up to that time, I was able to work in a way that allowed me to get as much off my desk as possible. In addition, it gave the person designated to fill in for me, plenty of time to organize their notes and thoughts and to ask questions in advance of the vacation. I was all set.

Naturally, time went by—months, weeks, days, hours, seconds and then I was finally living in the week of my scheduled and much-awaited family vacation.

As part of my very thorough preparation for the upcoming trip, I did what I always do.

Whenever I travel, I like to take off at least one day prior to the day of the actual trip. This is my standard, tried-and-true, one-day rule. This is my time to pack bags, then check and organize the house, my suitcase, and thoughts. That is my one-day-rule.

For this particular time and for good reason (at least I think), I thought (at the time I marked it on the calendar) I needed to take two days off prior to the trip. However, with the one-day rule firmly planted in mind, Wednesday came (which was two days before the departure) and rather than doing whatever it was that I planned to do on that extra day, I inadvertently went to work.

Technically, I did not blow the one-day-rule, but it seems I did waste some time on the day before (my day off where I erroneously went into work).

I was inadvertently thrown into a chaotic situation because even though I planned ahead and often while anticipating the trips, I failed to check my plan.

Similarity and Contrast

I read recently on the 'prevention.com' website that a person struggling with a hearing impairment or other inner ear issues might sometimes or suddenly feel unsteady or off balance in some situations.

The article explained that there are five, hair-like sensors in the inner ear that manage balance.

While far from being a scientist, and yet with the little bit that I do apprehend, I believe that I can form a reasonable opinion that the human body is an awesome organism and that we are all fearfully and wonderfully made despite what might seem some obvious flaws in the packaging.[vii]

And, despite the packaging, we should be in tune with the spirit of God and recognize the fact that He is still speaking.

Like those five, hair-like sensors that manage balance in the inner ear, when we neglect the voice or leading of the Spirit, then we will be thrown off balance.

When something seems out of whack, it might be best to stop and check things out because if you have prayed about it in advance, the Spirit of God might be trying to tell you something.

Therefore, do not neglect to listen to that small, still voice.[viii]

Balance

On that fateful Wednesday (planned vacation day), I, as usual, awakened to the annoying buzzing, beeping, and ringing all-at-once sound of my antiquated, digital alarm clock. I proceeded with my normal morning routine—watching the news on television, listening to the Steve Harvey Morning Show on the radio, showering, fixing my hair, putting on clothes and make-up, making my bed then finally leaving for work. All the while, something seemed a little off.

Oh, but it was a great day.

I was able to get ready and out of the house a little earlier than normal.

Yes, it was a great day indeed.

I had fewer fits of road rage because I could drive a little slower and did not have to navigate through traffic to maneuver around the barely-at-speed-limit drivers who in their quiet aggression clog up the fast lane on the highway.

In fact, even before getting to the highway—which is a few miles down the road and around the way—every traffic signal was green in my favor and I sailed through without ever having to stop.

Yes, but something seemed out of whack.

Scale/Proportion

It was a great day…it seemed better than most. In fact, it could not start any better.

Just one more day before I can sleep-in just a little bit later…oh yes, and to get lots of stuff done before we hit the road.

Normally, I run a bit late, so it was a huge, big deal making it to work a few minutes earlier than normal.

As I was pulling into the parking lot, someone from the third shift was pulling out of a parking space located close to the building, leaving a clear shot to get there before anybody else.

I thanked God for favor (we know favor isn't fair) and zipped into that 'prime' parking spot, which I knew without a shadow of a doubt that the good Lord, at that particular time on that particular day, created just for me.

Yet, even so, something seemed a little off.

Finally at my desk after having stopped at the kiosk for coffee and donuts and still listening through stereo headphones and enjoying the comedy of the Steve Harvey Morning Show, I was powering up my computer and starting the various applications so I can start the day at work; but I still just did not feel right.

About an hour later, my manager passed by my desk, first once and then again.

"Good morning," I smiled.

"Good morning," she said.

She then continued, "I thought you were off today."

Oh, what a beautiful day…and even though it just did not feel right, I said, "Not today but Thursday and Friday."

"Okay," she said as she walked away. It is a beautiful morning. I'm here a little earlier than normal, my manager saw me, so she thinks I'm a great, dedicated employee.

Surely, I will get at least one brownie point for the day. And on top of all of that, I do not have that many contracts to read through, yet.

It is a great day, but something is amiss.

I continued doing my work and at least another half an hour passed before a coworker walked by and said, "I thought you were supposed to be out on vacation today."

"Hmmm," I said as he walked away.

That did it! I pulled up the calendar to take a look.

Sure enough, protesting loudly and to the amusement of all whom happened to be within reach of my astonished proclamation, I screeched: "I AM SUPPOSED TO BE ON VACATION TODAY!"

Perspective

Reliving the events of that morning, it becomes more apparent that the whole situation turned out to be a lesson on keeping things in the proper perspective and intentionally choosing how to best mentally frame and reframe situations to create the best and most positive outcome.

If I were to assess the day with an unfitting perspective and not search for a reason to find joy or something for which to be grateful in the end, then it was, indeed, a terrible day.

I had so much to do but instead wasted a couple of hours getting dressed and then about another 45 minutes on the commute, parking, getting coffee and finally making it to my desk. Now I will have to spend another 45 minutes in the reverse trip back home.

I knew something was off!

Alternatively, by intentionally changing perspective and looking for the good in the events of that day in total, there are many reasons to celebrate.

There is reason to celebrate the fact that I arrived at work earlier, happier, and more stress-free than ever before.

There is reason to celebrate the fact that the roundtrip in to work and back home was without incident; I still got back home, packed and situated with reasonable good timing, and we left for the trip as planned and had a safe and wonderful time.

Moreover, there is reason to celebrate the lesson learned about how the aspirations and busyness of life (everything that we want and try to pack into a day or a life as a matter of course, comfort, or convenience) sets us up for some interesting challenges and consequences, which could really stress out an unprepared mind.

I am reminded of a very humorous television commercial about a product that does not readily come to mind. This fella (Jack) is introduced—'Meet Jack'.

As the narrator talks about all of his recently acquired possessions (perhaps a big new home, membership in an elite country club, kid applying for an Ivy League college), Jack is riding in circles on his mower, and cutting the grass of what appears to be a massive lawn.

As Jack's family is visible in the background celebrating in front of a rather large, expensive looking home, Jack (with a wide-eyed, uncomfortable grin plastered on his face) is waving to the camera in what appears to be poorly masked, overwhelmed desperation. Or, in other words, stressed.

Poor Jack!

The worst thing to come from showing up for work on a scheduled day off is that, that day has now gone down in infamy and remains a recurring joke during many office gatherings.

In reality, it is not that bad.

Laughter is good medicine for the heart, and we should all enjoy a good laugh every now and again.

Focal Point

It is common practice for skilled decorators and designers to build an incredibly beautiful and functional room around an eye-catching focal point.

A great focal point is one which naturally attracts the eye and highlights the room's best feature. It helps to set the mood of the room.

It could serve as the key for building an attractive and cohesive color scheme.

Moreover, it connects all the elements of the room and gives it a 'voice'.

Finding that voice in our living room could possibly be the most important point of this exercise.

Finding, hearing, and submitting to that voice means that we are connected to our higher source.

This Source connects all the elements of our lives.

Lest anyone is confused, the voice of our living room of life is not an audible one; it is an intuitive one.

It does not cause turmoil, but it aligns to the will of God and brings peace.

Moreover, it gives direction and provides assurance when we are on the right course, or chastisement when we are not.

When I was a kid, I remember thinking that anyone over the age of thirty was old.

If I came across someone forty, fifty, sixty years of age or more, then I felt sorry for them, thinking they were too old and feeble to do anything for themselves. They were elderly; they were or old.

June and Ward Cleaver, parents on the 1960s television show, 'Leave it to Beaver' were probably in their thirties, but to us as kids, they were old.

A few years later, Maude and her crew came on the scene with their wit and shenanigans.

They were in their fifties—we were still young, and they were still old.

However, we were probably thinking more along the lines of, "they are pretty old, but they are so cool.'

Years passed, then the 'Golden Girls' came along, and it was all over. Nobody is cooler than is a senior adult.

Growing up, I recall rations of scolding (or stern, sage advice) coming from the cool folk whether at home, at school, around the neighborhood or at church.

I particularly love the advice from the older, southern leaning folk especially at church. They would say stuff like, "you should alway follow yo' first mind".

Well, what they knew and what experience has since taught is that the 'first mind' about which they often spoke is not only that of our natural instincts but also and more importantly that of the 'small, still voice of God'.

Most of us have some memory of being in a situation where there was possibly a big deal decision to make.

Maybe during the situation, we got a fleeting glance—a feeling, a sense of a clear, concise answer or what seemed like divine direction—about which way to choose.

However, rather than entertain our higher thought, we immediately dismissed it and second-guessed or questioned ourselves.

We made a choice and chose to go left and then found that we should have chosen to go right.

Now we are lost!

In the case of my showing up for work on an off day, something did not seem right about that Wednesday morning, but instead of listening to that still small voice, I drowned it out with television, radio and the busyness of that day.

Even though there were wonderful lessons learned that day, in reflection, had I focused on making the day great—starting with prayer and meditation—rather than on simply having a great day, then that adventurous Wednesday in July might have played out a bit differently.

Had I taken the time to make the right connections and follow that 'still voice' that was signaling that something was not right, then maybe things would have gone a little differently.

Still of the Moment

For we walk by faith and not by sight,
The words that we believe and say.
But what we believe is not what we practice,
Sometimes when we start our day.
We awake from our slumber thankful,
But with a wince, a sign, and a frown.
Then jolt out of bed to start a new day,
Only to let new worries weigh us down.
But we walk by faith and not by sight,
This is what we believe.
Then why do we continue to expect the worst,
When God said, "Ask and you shall receive"?
Distracted by thoughts and issues,
As we plan and plot our day.
We are still neglecting to see the Father,
Who surely, has something to say.
But we walk by faith and not by sight,
So, where is our peace of mind?
He says to us in His small still voice,
My child, "If you seek then you will find".
Thoughts in our heads, worries on our minds,
Deadlines to meet and cope with,
He reminds us again in His still small voice,
If you would only knock, the door will be opened.
In the still of the moment in a beautiful quiet place,
We finally hear His voice and take heed.
He said, 'Be anxious for nothing and in every situation,
Start with prayer and you will succeed'.
In Christ Jesus,
Amen.

DIY Tips & Trick of the Trade
Creating a Focal Point

To create a great focal point that will work well in a space that has no built-in or structural interest, consider your favorite thing. It could literally be anything—a picture or some other piece of art, a rug, a piece of furniture, or simply something from your closet or even something from your yard or garage.

For instance, a focal point could be a collection of hats from your travels around the world. Make it interesting by arranging the hats in the shape of a state or world map.

The focal point could be a painted wall, painted in a different (yet compatible) eye-catching color. To that wall, add items of interest or even printed words, phrases or poems that will stimulate the senses and create a visual conversation about the room.

In addition, the focal point could be created by using lighting. Consider placing up or down lighting (maybe even in an accent color) round a beautiful, exotic plant or other items that you are proud to put on display.

In any case, the focal point should be attractive and compatible with the theme, tone, and mood of the room; however, try not to overdo it. While the focal point should make a statement, it should not overshadow all of the other elements in the room.
Whatever you choose, make it personal and proportionately powerful.

CHAPTER 5

The Elements of Design

The elements of interior design are expressed in various components, mediums and factors that are operated upon in a defined space to create, influence or achieve a desired look and feel.

The elements are value, shape, direction, color, texture, size and line.

Each element might mistakenly seem inconsequential when examined individually; however, each in its own unique way contributes to and powerfully impacts overall.

Trompe L'Oeil: "Trick the Eye"

In interior design, the term trompe l'oeil (tromp 'loi) is a term used to describe an art technique where the artist uses all of the elements of design to create a three-dimensional optional illusion.

Using this technique the artist might create something as simple as the illusion of a Black Widow spider spinning a massive web and crawling out of a deep, dark hole in a crumbling brick wall; or as intricate as a massive, foaming waterfall billowing in the middle of a street with marine life, large and small, swimming underneath.

However, no matter how ominous, exciting, and/or beautiful the image might appear, the one thing to be sure of is that it is not real.

In these situations, we count on our senses, rationale, and logic to work in tandem to assure us that we are safe.

Therefore, we can rest assured that the spider will not bite, and we will not drown in a body of water in the middle of the boulevard.

Tricks of the Traitor

We get bombarded, daily, by many people and issues, and face making decisions and choices about a myriad of everyday things.

The decisions and choices are based on a culmination of consequences, character, tendencies, and influence—either of our own, or of our perceptions of others who are affected or involved.

Those, though not exclusively, are the elements of our living room of life.

The traitor operates upon these elements. While it is not prudent and we cannot always use Flip Wilson's 'Geraldine' character's line, "The devil made me do it" to explain away bad acts or troubling situations; it is rather obvious when he is at work.

A few telltale signs are possibly evidenced whenever we allow a minor mince of words or disagreement to explode into a full-blown argument and misunderstanding; or an unreasonable phobia or the fear of the unknown to rob us of our joy or of what could very well be for us a-once-in-a-lifetime experience.

Further, we might allow a mere glance or subtle gesture from another person to either provoke us to anger or cause us to imagine an attraction that is not there or should never happen.

We might permit and unsubstantiated rumor whispered into our itchy ears to be the basis for which we form very important opinions or arrive at senseless conclusions.

Additionally, and maybe more laughable, if we read a note from a person, known or unknown, WHICH HAPPENS TO BE TYPED IN ALL CAPS; rather than believing that we are at the mercy of a languid or unskilled keyboardist, we might interpret the typeface as an inference of rage, hostility or some other form of aggression.

On occasion, maybe the arguments, phobias, fears, looks, gestures, rumors, or inferences have probable cause; however more often than not, they, like trompe-l'oeil, are simply illusions created by the author of confusion whose mission in life—and death—is to recraft the desired, created order into a convoluted mesh of chaos and commotion.

The traitor has slipped into our living room of life with his bag of tricks.

While he is there unpacking and deranging our thoughts and emotions, we might not be able to use the same sense and rationale we used when looking at the hypothetical painted art.

We might not be able to process the dilemmas of life and deal effectively with what is going on before us.

Instead, with our senses under siege and our room cluttered with his mess, we are in a reverse mode and are possibly reacting first and rationalizing later.

This only makes things worse and before we know it, we are in a situation or an all-out war over something that makes no sense.

This would be much the same as accepting his persuading that the afore-mentioned trompe l'oeil illustrations are real: that the spider is going to bite; we are going to drown in the middle of the road; it's doomsday and we are all going to die-- when in fact, all it is, is simply a mind game.

The antithesis of this is that whenever we are in those diverse situations and recognize that we are in need of a 'more better' understanding, it might benefit us greatly to think with our whole hearts rather than our hard heads.

We must do this all while trusting and believing that the Master Designer is working on our behalf and for His own good.

He will, in his perfect timing, calm the raging storms, bring inner peace, right the wrongs and make our paths straight.[ix]

DIY Tips & Tricks of the Trade:

Cozy Color, Comfy Space

Color is very important in interior design because it: 1) sets the visual atmosphere, 2) subconsciously affects our feelings, and 3) could easily help to facilitate a nice quick and inexpensive change to a room from season to another.

A skillful and intentional use of color could serve not only as a tool to turn a series of rooms into a home, but it also could save the home decorator the expense of buying additional furniture or accessories to fill a void.

A fun fact about color is that just like in physics, neither Black nor White are consider "colors" in the design world. Yet, they are particularly useful tools to use along with the color pallet.

However, for those of us who fall in love with and fully appreciate the clean, crisp, and airy look and feel of a white-on-white room, there is no need to panic—it is allowed and achievable.

To pull this off skillfully and beautifully, we should do lots of research and then trust our instincts to choose a suitable foundation then layer it with a variety of fun, funky textures, tints, and tones.

Conversely, for those of us who enjoy being more adventurous, bold, and walking on the wild side, we can certainly build a scheme around Black and command it to 'shine'.

This effort would probably take a little more research and skill to pull off than the White; however, it can be done.

If we want to experiment with Black walls, then we must absolutely make sure that the space is flooded with lots of natural light. Make the trim bright white and for our furniture we could use graduating tones of gray, interesting patterns, exotic, skin prints, and bold and bright pops of color.

We should also consider using lots of greenery and beautiful wood tones or treatments.

SIPPING TEA IN THE LIVING ROOM

This approach will not only add interest to the space, it would help to make sure that the feel of the room is not like the dread of a dungeon.

There was a time it was considered taboo to have the walls painted a different color for each room in the house; but not so much anymore.

If we decide we cannot live without color.

If we want to fill our home with it while at the same time still wanting our various spaces to look like we are in the same house as we go from one room to the next.

The simple thing that we could do is to consider picking a compatible accent color and finding a clever way to use it in proportion in every room (i.e., an accent wall in the living room; towels in the bathroom; a centerpiece on the dining room table, canisters on the kitchen counter; lampshades in the bedroom).

The possibilities are almost as endless as our imaginations.

We should not be afraid to use the colors we love. If there is a question about how to put them together, the easiest thing to do is to visit a local paint or hardware store and study or use the color pallets suggested by the paint manufacturers.

And for inspiration, for instance, find a picture or a piece of art that you admire.

Study how the artist (who is expert in using and combining colors) distributes the colors in the piece.

Pay attention to and get a feel for which colors repeat or which ones pop and in what proportion.

Then, if you can, imagine the colors on your walls, floors, furniture, and accent pieces in those proportions.

This exercise will go a long way in helping to achieve a pleasant distribution of color and an aesthetically beautiful, balanced feeling room.

CHAPTER 6

Furnishing the Room:

When Size Really Does Not Matter

When my mom, in her later years, was preparing to move out of the family home to a substantially smaller apartment in a senior villa, we had a really fun debate about whether or not she should take all of the pieces of her bedroom set with her or leave a few pieces behind.

"Momma", I said, backed up with all of my training, "all of that stuff is not going to fit into the bedroom of your new apartment; you should consider leaving some of it behind."

"Yes, it will," she said, quite amused.

"No, momma, it's not going to fit."

Again, she demanded, "yes, it will fit."

Once again, I stubbornly insisted that, "all of that furniture is not going to fit into that space; you should consider leaving some of it behind".

To this she responded sternly in her deep southern dialect with only two words: "mejsha it!"

Okay, the challenge was on; I was about to prove my mother wrong.

So out comes the measuring tape, pencils, and grid paper. I proceed to carefully measure, plot and draw the room and furniture to scale. When the drawing was complete, I said, "See momma, the furniture is too big; you will not have much room to walk around."

My mother studied the neatly drawn illustration for a few minutes and then asked, "What's this?" as she pointed to what appeared to be narrow paths in and around the room.

"A walkway," I said. "So, I can walk from here to here, right?"

"Yes ma'am," I replied.

"And I can walk from here to here, right?" She asked quite wittingly.

"Yes ma'am, but you will have limited space."

To this she quipped, "I need a place to sleep and to store my possessions; not a place to throw a party. If I can do those things in that room with that furniture, then

I'm taking all of it with me and all of it is going in the room. Case closed."

"Yes ma'am, we're gonna make it work."

… and When it Does

I am not sure if there is anything really magical about buying furniture, but I do know that there are a few really important things that we should consider before making the purchase and they are these:

That beautiful furniture that we see on the showroom floor is really bigger than we think. Furniture showrooms are usually very large, open spaces with sky-high ceilings. And, though we might know that some pieces are amply sized, sometimes we will not be able to fully appreciate and comprehend the true breadth until we get it home to our 12x18 foot room with its 9 foot ceiling; and windows, pathways, doorways and HVAC vents everywhere.

When moving from a small apartment to a more spacious house, the furniture that once filled our cozy, neatly packed living room might really be smaller than we thought. This is another instance of the eye using space, size and proportion to play tricks on us. It is like seating a 6-foot tall adult in a chair meant for a preschool aged child: the adult looks massive while seated there. However, if we seated that same adult in a giant-sized chair at the carnival or fair, then that rather tall person would appear diminutive in size.

Considering the age and type of house, that beautiful oversized sofa might be larger than the doorway. It might be hard to believe but there are occasions when a lovely, older, Victorian style home might look lovely with a big beautiful contemporary sofa placed squarely in the middle of the living room floor. However, that is not what the designers and architects had in mind when the home was built. Therefore, the doorways or hallways might not be too receptive to the idea, and during the move, we might find it exceedingly difficult if not impossible to get very large pieces of furniture in place. This also might apply to some apartments and condos.

Even though some things have a way of working out for the best, when making a large purchase such as this we should be careful to remember that in the land of efficient decorating and design, measuring tape is still king.

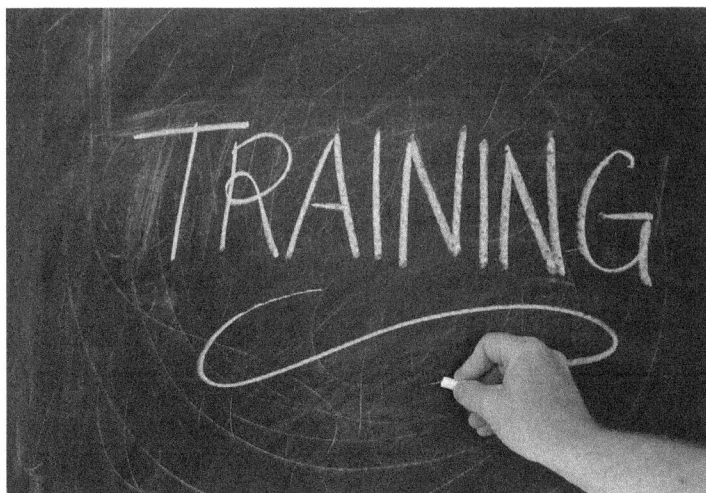

Sage Advice: Momma Was Right

On moving day, we packed up the bags, loaded up the trucks and headed to my mom's new apartment, which was just around the corner from the family home.

We did not bring much furniture from the house because in between signing the lease and moving day, we took her shopping and bought momma brand new furniture for the living room and a new dinette set.

After a couple of days, we managed to get everything set up and organized.

The apartment was beautiful—beautifully coordinated, beautifully arrange and just like home, beautifully filled with love—even the bedroom where, as it turned out, momma was right. The furniture fit in the room just fine.

From this I guess I not only gained a memory to hold on to for life and smile about whenever I think of my beloved mother, but I also learned that while there is absolutely nothing wrong with believing in myself, my education and training; there is also nothing wrong with being proven wrong or corrected by a more gifted person, who might not possess the same papers or letters as I, but is divinely seasoned to reach back and train up.

We all should be so lucky.[x]

Tips and Trick of the Trade

The Art of Placement Dos and Don'ts

There are a lot of things to take into consideration when arranging furniture in the living room if our goal is to create a space that is both visually attractive and physically comfortable.

Some of these include the size and shape of the room, the location of fixed items such as entryways, windows, vents, light switches, and electrical outlets.

In addition, there are the sometimes more subtle effects such as the direction and source of light, or the overall intended look and feel of the room.

With that in mind and without the luxury of a doing a one-on-one consultation and assessment, it might be best at this point to list the top 5 "do's" and "don'ts that might be helpful for a do-it-yourself (DIY) project.

Dos:

Start with a plan. If the goal is to update, we could consider changing out pillows or adding slipcover to what we already have.

If the plan is a major remodel, then we may need to consider the furniture in a wider plan, along with new paint, flooring, and window coverings.

Measure. The measuring tape is our friend. Measure, measure, measure: height, width, and depth.

Compatibility. Make sure that the furniture is compatible with the room in all aspects, including style, use, color and cost.

Showroom Effect. When shopping, we should remember that our furniture will probably look different in our home than it does in the store. Prepare for the best but save your receipts.

Personality. We should be sure to include and work around the things we really love

Don'ts:

Do not fall in line. Resist the urge to line furniture up against the walls. Angle the furniture against corners; create conversation pits and other groupings; float the furniture towards the middle or a focal point.

"If it don't fit, don't force it". Do not turn the room into an obstacle course. While it is possible to oversize a room with larger furniture to make it feel larger; however, if we go that route we should be sure to add fewer pieces and secure a logical and comfortable pathway in and around the room.

Do not match sets. Resist the urge of only picking matching sets. It looks great in the store but for added interest, try to mix things up a bit.

No blocking. We should, never, ever obscure an entryway unless there is more than one way into or out of the room (and even doing it then is questionable). Doing so would be sure to cause lots of unnecessary confusion.

Do not rush the project. Anything that is worth doing is worth doing right so if planning, measuring, shopping, and placing all wind up being more than a one weekend project, then so be it. The extra time invested will be so much   more   worth   it   in   the   end.

CHAPTER 7

Soft Furnishing: Windows and Rugs

Dressing the Windows

It is a beautiful, befitting analogy that just as windows are the eyes of our rooms, our eyes are the window of our soul. Both let in light, reveal darkness, and expose emptiness or purpose.

As covering for the eyes in a room, window treatments are so important that whenever we sell our home or move from one place to another, the treatments almost automatically become a fixture. They become part of the structure, and whether good or bad, they transfer with the title.

The downside of this is that if we move from one location to another, we might leave behind something that we love and acquire some treatments that we do not particularly like.

When considering the whole process of selecting, fitting, and installing the appropriate and beautiful window treatments, we could end up making a sizeable purchase. We, therefore, should sacrifice where we must and devote a good amount of time and resources to the endeavor.

As treatment for the eyes of our soul in our living room of life, there is no better covering than the precious blood of Jesus and the mighty word of God.

This treatment is universal and final. It required a great amount of planning, love, and sacrifice. And, because of the care that went into applying this covering, we should be more mindful of the eyes that are peering into our living room than the ones that are looking out.

In our living room of live, the eyes that are peering in are merciful, infallible, and searches for truth and commitment to the Master's Plan, while watching every step of the wicked and the good[xi].

The eyes looking out of the windows of our living room of life are well meaning but limited; they see but are never satisfied[xii].

With such a beautiful treatment as the covering of the Lord serving as covering for our soul, our living room of life should overflow with peace; have abundance of joy; and cast a bright light of hope.

Moreover, in our living room of life, we should endeavor to do justice, love mercy, and walk humbly before our Creator.[xiii]

And when we move from this place to the next (which will be our eternal home), there is one thing of which we can be sure: What we encounter on the other side will be more than we deserve and better than anything that we leave behind.

The Obstructed View

I remember sitting in church as a child, sometimes restless, sometimes secretly playing games with my siblings or other contemporaries, and sometimes actually listening to the Pastor deliver his fire and brimstone sermons.

In the African American Baptist tradition, it is always exciting to listen to and watch the orator as he preaches with passion, adding theatrics, sometimes over-the-top histrionics and soul-stirring whoops, hoops, and different inflections.

Yet, as a child or young adult, whatever the pastor preached about (outside of the prospect of burning in Hell), seemed to be of little interest or relevance to me.

In my mind, that was grown folk business.

However, there were times when he would tell a story that was interesting enough to make me pay attention.

During one of his sermons, to illustrate how we can sometimes misinterpret things because of our own sometimes-skewed views (to put it nicely), Pastor told a story about a well-meaning, nosey neighbor.

The woman, in fact, was a busybody who could not resist the urge to spy on and judge her neighbors while they were engaging in their normal, daily activities.

I still belong to the same church where I grew up and with many of the same people. Therefore, it is not uncommon to hear some of the same wisdom and stories shared by those who heard or succeeded him.

As I recall the story (and as I take the liberty of modifying it slightly to make it more relatable to modern-day sensibilities), this good but busybody woman was fixated on her neighbor's laundry, which was hanging outside on the lines to dry.

In fact, this was not just any laundry; it was the all-important 'white clothes', which included bed sheets, bath towels, underwear and the like.

I believe my ears were pricked for this story because for many of our neighbors and us, hanging clothes outside on the line to dry was not a luxury exercised in order to enjoy the sunshine freshness that the warm breezes would produce. It was a necessity because we had, neither, an electric nor gas clothes dryer on the inside.

However, as this modified story goes, the busybody spied on her neighbor and complained incessantly about how dingy the woman's wash looked.

In fact, the 'white clothes', in her mind, were so dingy that she felt ashamed for her neighbor.

The nosey woman prided herself on producing the best and the brightest white 'whites' and proudly put them on display.

On the days that she did not wash, she was on the inside looking out to see what the others were doing.

Without fail, whenever she looked out of her window and saw, she would complain.

She complained to anyone within range, including her husband, children, relatives, friends, and other neighbors.

She complained about looking out the window and seeing the neighbor's dingy laundry.

She had become obsessed with the view; she never got enough.

However, over time, the same people to whom she complained started whispering about her.

"What's really going on with Miss Mary?"

The problem for Mary was that no one who spent time outside of her house after the neighbor hanged her laundry, ever saw things from the Mary's point of view.

Finally, Mary's husband had enough and confronted her during one of her rants.

He said, "Honey, I know you put a lot of work and effort into keeping the house tidy, the children cared for, our meals cooked and our clothes clean. However, I've been busy putting in extra time at work; I could not adequately keep up with my chores."

He said, "Whenever I go out after our neighbor hangs her laundry, I find that the whites are so bright that they are blinding."

He continued, "After some investigating, I discovered that it is not that our neighbor's laundry is dingy; the real problem is that our windows are dirty".

Miss Mary learned a memorable and unbelievably valuable lesson that day.

So, did I by hearing this story, and hopefully, so do we all by reading and rehearsing it.

Rugs as Furnishings

Rugs are wonderful pieces that as furnishing can act as an island in a room where it is surrounded by the flooring of choice and nestled on top is usually an arrangement of tables or chairs, or simply the beauty of its own artful design.

Also, larger rugs can be used to visually divide a room of generous proportions into distinctive vignettes: a hip conversation pit as a centerpiece; a cozy sitting area in front of the fireplace; a relaxing reading nook by the window, and so on.

As accessories, smaller rugs are usually scattered about the room adding interesting pops of texture and color, or simply serving as a pretty, little mat to protect the flooring from the influence of outside elements.

However, whether as accessories or furnishings, rugs are great to have around but they are not mandatory. They simply serve when and where placed at the pleasure of the homeowner.

If we are to use them, though, we should make sure that they are coordinated with and suited for the room in regard to size, detail, purpose and cost.

We would never put an expensive rug at the entrance to the mud room nor a door mat under our beautifully arranged living room table.

Not Made to be an Island

In 1945, Alma Bazel Androzzo, a gifted but virtually unknown pianist, lyricist, and singer brilliantly composed and performed for the Tuberculosis Society, the affectionately known and much renowned hymn titled, 'If I Can Help Somebody Along the Way'.

This song is the battle cry of the benevolent among us. Those who are tugged and nudged to enlarge our territories and make our giving more magnanimous and our living more meaningful than for self, alone.

This song has been performed by many remarkable singers and ultimately was made famous by gospel music's great, Mahalia Jackson when she recorded it in 1951.

Another instance, which propelled it into the spotlight and rewarded it much acclaim, was when the illustrious Dr. Martin Luther King, Jr. quoted the verses in his almost prophetic, self-penned eulogy, which was (in due course) read at his funeral:

If I can help somebody as I pass along;

If I can cheer somebody with a word or song;

If I can show somebody he is traveling wrong;

Then my living shall not be in vain.

The sentiment felt through the words of this song makes it music to the ears of brave soldiers who serve at the pleasure of our Lord.

The words reverberate incessantly in the steadfast souls of trusted ambassadors who cherish the thought of being placed in position and having the freedom to choose each day how, whom, when, and what we will serve.

When we choose, we serve by spreading our gifts on the altar of humanity and being mindful of the fact that we are created to be a part of a whole rather than a splintered island off to itself.

We decide that we are best when we discipline our minds and train our thoughts on protecting the weak and valuing the most vulnerable around us.

In this way, we can more truthfully celebrate our noble calling and higher purpose as we (at His pleasure and through Him) actively become joy, peace, and love to what seems like a complex and dying world.

Otherwise, we do nothing more than look for schemes and chase the wind while continuing to question the meaning of life.xiv

DIY: Tips & Tricks of the Trade

Window Coverings

When it comes to window coverings, the styles are splendidly diverse, and the choices are virtually endless. The trick, then, is deciding how to best manage the investment—will this remain a well-managed, do-it-yourself project or is there room in the budget for acquiring the skills of an expert?

The simplest and budget-friendly (yet adorable) thing to do to windows in the living room, if we dare, is to add a topper and leave them bare. However, there are some "Yes's" and "No's" to consider before going this route are listed below.

Yes:

if doing so would expose and highlight beautiful millwork:

if doing so would not impede too much on privacy;

if doing so would not in any ways compromise safety.

No:

if doing so would expose the beautiful and valuable contents of the room to too much sunlight and thus, premature aging, wear, and tear; and

 if doing so is not compatible with the look, style and feel of the room itself.

In contrast, however, the most luxurious and relatively expensive-but well-worth-it thing to do is to call in the expert. With this method, a stylist would come into the home to make evaluations about the desires of the owner/occupant, the natural light allowances, and the style of the room and its furnishings. He or she will then take all proper and correct measurements. Finally, they will deliver and install a product that will be pleasing for many years to come.

This is the route to take if the window treatment is to be at least an intermediate to life-term investment, where no matter what else changes in the room, the windows will remain dressed in this same manner for at least 5 years and as many as 10-15 (the time when homeowners typically reinvest and make major changes).

There are many other avenues to explore between these two extremes that would certainly do the trick such as:

the skillful use of beautiful, ready-made scarves, curtains and drapery;

mini, plantation blinds, or vertical blinds; or simply, the artful use of some irresistible fabric found on a clearance table.

We are in a time when for the masses, self-expression means more than falling in line with old standards and expectations. However, whenever we are making such an important choice as this, we should be careful to choose wisely because most people will only see our home looking from the outside in.

A beautifully furnished home with unsightly window treatments detracts from our home's perceived value and attractiveness.

CHAPTER 8

Accessorizing for a Beautiful Finish

In the world of interior design, the key to a beautifully decorated room is adding finishing touches for maximum effect. The key to adding these wow-inspiring touches is to add accessories that might build around a theme or a one wow-inspiring thing. An exciting idea for this might include popping in playful wisps of color, inspired art, or treasured objects of interesting shapes, sizes, or subject matter.

Accessories take on many wonderful forms for our visual pleasure including photographs, paintings, metals and other wall art, vases, baskets, florals, books, and other trinkets and treasures. The list goes on. And for our creature comfort we might consider pillows, lamps, throws and even a whimsical or exotic footstool. These all help to establish an intentional and well thought out finished look and feel for our decor.

At this point in our project, after all planning, purchasing and placement are complete, this is a great time to experiment with a variety of things to create the magic and added fun.

Now is the time to play around with different levels of excitement and before we know it, even the simplest of rooms has a radiant personality reflective of the mood, tastes, and values of its owner / occupant.

We are now closer than ever to the point where we can kick up our heels, pat ourselves on the back and say, 'well done'.

Mirror as Accessory and Tool

A mirror is one of most basic and the universally used accessories in home décor because not only does it help to spark up and add life to most any space, we rely on and use it as a tool for self-assessment.

The basic function of a conventional mirror is to reflect whatever is put before it. If light is put before it, then light is reflected. If it sits amid darkness, then darkness prevails. If beauty makes a bow, then loveliness applauds and fills the space. And, consequently, if ugliness is afore, then unpleasantness is returned.

As an accessory, a beautiful mirror when smartly placed gives the impression of spaciousness and light, and it creates the subliminal sense of rhythm and repetition that is often desired and present in good design. It is an asset used to elegantly fill and warm an otherwise cold and lonely wall.

As a tool, the mirror is a force with which we reckon daily. Think of how many times a day (good, bad, or ugly) that we see the images of ourselves through the lens of any form of mirror or reflector.

As part of our daily routine, many of us, at the sound of the alarm, bolt out of bed in the morning and stumble into the bathroom.

There we are almost surely greeted by at least one mirror, and in it, we see the often-unappreciated beauty of our morning face.

Then after we scrub, clean, paint, fix, and put everything together, we check the mirror one last time to see how we are doing before we leave home heading out for our day.

Afterwards, when we set ourselves in motion and find ourselves walking to and from the parking lot, a bus stop, a train, or whatever our mode of transportation, we are forced to evaluate ourselves, yet again, when we see our reflections peeking through another shiny object—a window, the shiny trim around the doorways, or an elevator door.

The images from many of these objects are not true reflections but rather are distorted representations of ourselves. These are those which make us think we are either looking better than we really are, or not so good.

Judging by what we see, we confirm with our distorted selves that our day is going to either be extremely good, or extremely bad—never just okay.

Unfortunately, upon this false premise we might sadly, base our mood or construct our day.

As Divine Inspiration

Picture this: You are having a good day. You wake up in the morning thanking the Lord for another day and pledging to do good, love mercy and walk humbly before Him, and all of that.[xv]

You are humming along, knocking out one project after another, and quietly affirming to yourself that you are blessed, highly favored, and walking in the goodness of the Lord.

Then—in what seems like from out of nowhere— halfway through the day—BAM!—you are met with what feels like a double dose of rudeness, unkindness and outright meanness from someone in your personal space!

What to do? What to do?

Some things happen inside you: each action causing an unkind reaction.

You suddenly find you are spending the remainder of this day feeling extremely remorseful first, about going off on a super nice customer service representative at the cable company; and after that, snapping at a coworker who had the temerity to pop in (not once but twice) to ask a question while you are in the middle of your crisis.

However, thankfully, from a calm, deep place you are reminded of not only what to do, but also of what not to do.

At times like these, while still in the growth and development (or accessorizing) phase, we might find that we allow some things in our living room of life that should not exist.

And, using a common term used in decorating or design to describe the situation, it could be said that we are accessorizing with trappings that are incompatible with the life that we are striving to live.

These type trappings provide neither pleasure nor comfort, but instead promote stress and 'dis-ease'.

No matter how well camouflaged or cute they appear, they are anger, envy, sorrow, regret, greed, arrogance, self-pity, guilt, resentment, inferiority, lies, false pride, ego and superiority.

Moreover, if we are not careful, we will find that these encumbrances are powerful foes and usually operate in sets of threes. For instance, greed begets envy, which begets resentment. This goes on and on.

So, what to do, what to do the next time that life delivers a "BAM" moment?

As for me, I hope I am reminded as much as I was convicted to look outside of myself and to another source for reflection, and for this, there is no better accessory in this space than the ever-fresh, living word of God.

The Word of God operates the same as our conventional mirror, only the reflections are perfected, and the images are true because no matter what is put before it, it reflects His beautiful truths.

If doubt is put before it, assurance is mirrored. If hate is put before it, then love is exposed. If a lie is put before it, then rest assured that the truth is returned.

Moreover, if we dare put ourselves before the perfect mirror of the mighty word of God, then our sinful selves masked by the love, saving grace and abundant mercy of God, our Lord and Savior is manifested and springs forth the possibility of joy, peace, hope, serenity, humility, kindness, benevolence, empathy, generosity, compassion and faith.

I did not have an opportunity to apologize to the customer service representative that day, but was convicted and therefore compelled to set things right with my coworker—who, with or without an apology, remained as determined as ever to finish the project as she set out to do.

Tip and Trick of the Trade

The Power of Vignettes

Creating vignettes or table-scaping is a beautiful and creative way of showcasing accessories in our living room. This method allows us to:

- centralize our collections;

- add different areas of interest within the room; and

- avoid the possibility of our trinkets and treasures looking more like clutter than thoughtful design.

Consider the following scenario: You have an interesting collection of figurines that boast of your travels. You are very fond of them and you want to put them on display throughout the room.

Instead of this: Scattering the figurines around the room—some on the coffee table, some on the mantle, some on the bookshelf, and then some more possibly on each end table;

Try this: Find a spot in the room—for instance a bookshelf, and intentionally place the figurines on and around the shelves, interweaving them with the books and surrounding them by other items as if to tell a story.

To make the artfully arranged vignette more interesting, it is a good idea to work with odd sets of components, totaling more than one (i.e. 3 items; or 5 items).

The items should be of varying sizes or textures, (i.e. three pillows on the end of a sofa—a textured one, one of a different orientation, and one that makes a statement with a word or an initial.)

And, the arrangement should appear, not so much as a focal point (though we could certainly use this as such), but as a beautiful image set against the larger backdrop.

This method works well no matter if you are adding pillows to a sofa, pictures, trinkets, or treasures on a table, or accent pieces on the floor next to the hearth. The items placed should complement each other in terms of subject, size and proportion, and the grouping should make sense.

Nevertheless, now is the time to let creativity flow. So, go ahead and arrange, rearrange, and arrange again, then step back and look at the creation to see how it makes you feel.

Next, for a fresher perspective, turn around, walk out of the room, count to ten, come back, and take another look around.

At this point, you will either feel really satisfied or you might feel the need to start over. In the case of an epic fail (which surely will not happen) some might feel the need to call a friend.

Unnecessary Clutter

The good thing about a significant home decorating project is that during the process we are forced, or at least encouraged, to reckon with and possibly purge unnecessary stuff.

Stuff can take on many forms. It can be anything from the out of date trinkets that are collecting dust behind the glass of the entertainment center; to the now under-stuffed pillows, which doubled as a headrest on those evenings when watching television turned into an overnight event; to the bags and boxes of "important" papers that have not seen the light of day since they were dropped there more than a year or two ago.

Stuff can detract from the overall appearance of the room. It can clog valuable nooks and corners that crave the experience of hosting a beautiful statement piece that could perk up the room.

Moreover, the presence of stuff (or even just the mere thought of having to deal with it) can prove overwhelming.

Though now, presenting itself in the form of unnecessary clutter, stuff once had a place but has since, served its purpose. Now, it is time to review, release and renew.

They! Baggage; Not Mine

Sometimes we unwittingly invite others into the nooks and crannies of our deeply personal space and soon after crossing the threshold (much to our dismay), 'They' drop into to the recesses of our minds with their tattered baggage filled with short sightedness, disbelief, prophecies of doom and gloom, the 'no we can't' disorder, the 'if I hadda, coulda, woulda, shoulda' syndrome, and worst of all, the 'They said' blues.

So, who are 'They'?

As someone who is familiar to us, 'They' might be the person or persons living in our home, or who might stop in for a visit from time-to-time stop.

'They' might share an office space or work in a cubicle down the row.

'They' might attend the same schools or classes; or might even teach in them.

'They' might occupy the adjoining seats at church on Sunday mornings, share in a ministry, or sit on the same committee.

As someone who feels the need to counsel us, 'They' are the ones who, though disguising their statements as questions, love to be heard as they slyly suggest that there is another way.

In all of their subtlety they loudly and poignantly point out what is wrong with your religion; what is wrong with your thinking; what is wrong with your church; what is wrong with your faith; and moreover what is simply wrong with you and why you do not measure up.

As someone who wishes to teach us, 'They' will punish you for what you know, and for what you do not know.

'They' judge according to their own successes and failures, not fully understanding the implication of doing either.

Furthermore, in their minds, they alone grasp and have a firm hold on all things and speak according to their own worldly wisdom and puffed up knowledge.

As someone who might be highly esteemed by others, 'They' have standards that are so high that, though they may not realize it, they themselves cannot attain them. They have lofty dreams and selfish goals. They have bought into the idea that the world is their oyster and they are lying in their beds being perfected and shaped into beautiful pearls; or that the world is their stage and they have indomitably willed that not anything or anybody will upstage them.

As someone who wishes to judge us, 'They' have keen foresight yet lack insight, and is oblivious to hindsight. They are apt to find every flaw in a near-perfect diamond as well as the smallest spot on a black tarp in the dark.

As someone who clearly does not have a clue, 'They' pray to God and are therefore the only ones whom He hears or will speak to and through about everybody's business but their own. In addition, forgetting that the Word says that our days on this earth will be short and full of trouble, they mistakenly believe that because they are not presently in a storm, they are more blessed than the ones who might have gotten caught up and are now fighting for their lives.[xvi]

Lastly, as someone witnessing the blessings of the Lord in our favor, 'They' secretly conspire to shrink our territory, stunt our growth, and keep us from reaching our God-given potential by patting us on the back while holding out hope that our next step will lead to a stumble and a fall.

'They' are wounded and misguided carpenters, working with the wrong tools and building walls destined to hem themselves in and all around.

Moreover, and sadly, without the proper perspective, on any given day, 'They' could be any one of us.

Therefore, it should behoove us to guard the doors of our hearts, protect the windows of our minds and turn on the watch light of or our soul so that 'They' cannot fill our living room of life with unnecessary clutter.

For the sake of the more perfect Plan for our lives, 'They' baggage must be left on the stoop on the other side of the door.

CHAPTER 10

Voile! It is Finished

The one thing that really gives me great joy in my living room is knowing that by His grace and my choice, the Spirit of God resides here as my counselor and comforter. It is only by His grace and mercy that I can say that my life is complete in Him.

Therefore, whenever it seems like things are not working out according to plans, and I feel I'm being bombarded by influences outside of my control or even swayed by my own senses and emotions within, I can look to find solace in the One who walks beside me every step of the way and who lavishes me with love and forgiveness; who guides me with divine direction, pampers me with peace and who generously changes my error and brokenness into another chance.

By His grace, my living room is complete. I am glad to say that even though there are still some things that need to be worked out, arranged, repaired, replaced, and perfected, the heavy lifting was done on the cross. It is finished.

HOPE

My hope is built on nothing less

than Jesus' blood and righteousness.

I dare not trust the sweetest frame,

but wholly lean on Jesus' name.

It's on Christ the solid rock I stand;

all other ground is sinking sand.

(My Hope Is Built on Nothing Less – Edward

Mote, 1797 – 1874)

ABOUT THE AUTHOR

T. T. Carole is a business professional with a background and training in the corporate world as well as interior design, religious studies, teaching, women's ministry, and lifestyle coaching.

She has degrees in Interdisciplinary Studies (Columbia College, Missouri), and Ministry and Leadership (Missouri Baptist University), as well as various diplomas and certifications in interior decorating, Leadership Teaching and Training (ETA), and Women's Ministry (Light University).

This book is the first of a 5 books in her planned series, which she has titled: DESIGNED FOR LIFE.

NOTES

[i] "And we know that in all things God works for the good of those who love him, who have been called according to his purpose." (Romans 8:28)

[ii] "But if serving the LORD seems desirable to you, then choose for yourselves this day whom you will serve, whether the gods your ancestors served beyond Euphrates, or the gods of the Amorites, in whose land you are living. But as for me and my household, we will serve the LORD." (Joshua 24:14-15, NIV)

[iii] 1 Timothy 6 – (The Message Bible)

[iv] "For I know the plans I have for you," declares the LORD, "plans to prosper you and not harm you, plans to give you hope and a future." (Jeremiah 29:11, NIV)

[v] Romans 8:28 (see 'i' above)

[vi] Nehemiah said, "Go and enjoy choice food and sweet drinks, and send some to those who have nothing prepared. This day is holy to our Lord. Do not grieve, for the joy of the LORD is your strength." (Nehemiah 8:10, NIV)

[vii] "I praise you because I am fearfully and wonderfully made; your works are wonderful, I know that full well." (Psalm 139:14, NIV)

[viii] "After the earthquake came a fire, but the LORD was not in the fire. And after the fire came a gentle whisper." (1 Kings 19:12,

NIV)

ix "Trust in the LORD with all your heart and lean not on your own understanding; in all your ways submit to him, and he will make your paths straight." (Proverbs 3:5-6, NIV)

x "Train up a child in the way he should go: and when he is old, he will not depart from it." (Proverbs 22:6, KJV); and "Likewise, teach the older women to be reverent in the way they live, not to be slanderers or addicted to much wine, but to teach what is good. Then they can urge the younger women to love their husbands and children, to be self-controlled and pure, to be busy at home, to be kind, and to be subject to their husbands so that no one will malign the word of God." (Titus 2:3-5)

xi "the eyes of the LORD are everywhere, keeping watch on the wicked and the good." (Proverbs 15:3)
xii "Death and Destruction are never satisfied, and neither are human eyes." (Proverbs 27:20)
xiii "He has shown you, O mortal, what is good. And what does the Lord require of you? To act justly and to love mercy and to walk humbly with your God." (Micah 6:8, NIV)

xiv "Fools fold their hands and ruin themselves. Better one handful with tranquility than two handfuls with toil and chasing after the wind." (Ecclesiastes 4:5-6, NIV)

xv Micah 6:8 (see 'xi' above)

xvi "Mortals, born of woman, are of few days and full of trouble." (Job 14:1, NIV)

www.ingramcontent.com/pod-product-compliance
Lightning Source LLC
Chambersburg PA
CBHW031535040426
42445CB00010B/549